SIGHT READING
PIANO 5
GRADE
MALCOLM RILEY & PAUL TERRY

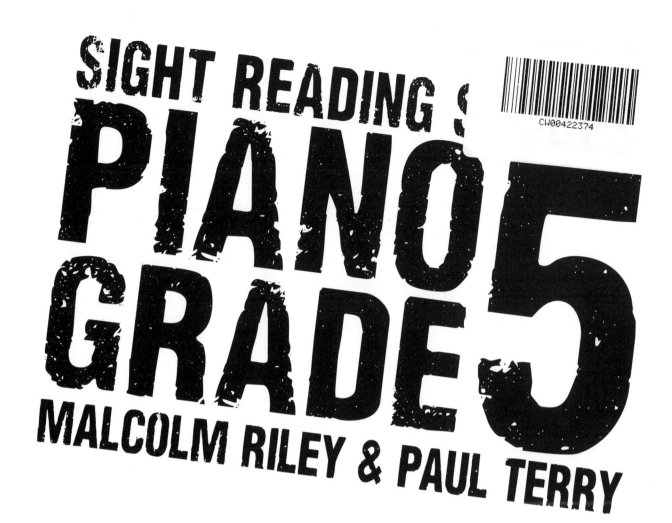

RHINEGOLD
EDUCATION

WWW.RHINEGOLDEDUCATION.CO.UK

FOR STUDENTS

Sight reading is an important and enjoyable musical skill. The more you practise the better you will get, and working carefully through this book will help you.

Use the CD included with this book to hear how the pieces should sound. Listen to the music carefully to check your playing. Most of the written instructions are also spoken for you on the CD. The tracks can be downloaded onto an MP3 player if you find that easier to use next to the piano.

From the beginning of the book to piece 10 you should listen to the recording of each piece first to hear how it should sound (except when you are asked to do otherwise). Then play the music on the piano, copying what you have heard. From piece 12 onwards, make sure that you play first and then listen to check that you were correct. Up to piece 34 there are spoken reminders about important things to notice in the music, but after that you are on your own!

Tick the box when you have finished each section or piece, so that you know which ones you have tried – it's not sight reading if you keep playing the same pieces!

If you find any of the examples on the CD are too fast when you are starting out, there are software programs available on the internet that can slow down the speed of music on any CD played on a computer. One that is free to download is: **Speedshifter** (available from www.abrsm.org/en/students/speedshifter).

FOR TEACHERS

This book follows the sight reading requirements for the Grade 5 piano exam of the Associated Board of the Royal Schools of Music (as revised in 2009). It is also suitable for all piano students who wish to improve their sight reading skills.

A unique feature of the books in this series is the inclusion of a specially-recorded CD which students can use at home for additional guidance, and to check the accuracy of their own playing. Encourage your students to use it as a tool to evaluate their own playing and learn from their mistakes, as well as a support for when you are not there to help.

Sight Reading Success progressively introduces each of the elements in sight reading, along with many useful tips and exercises to improve fluency. Each book builds on the skills taught in the previous volumes, so it is recommended that your students work through Grades 1, 2, 3 and 4 before starting on this book.

The second part of the book includes exam-standard pieces to play in lessons or at home. Take a few minutes in every lesson to check progress and help with any difficulties, and encourage regular sight reading so that students have confidence when going into their exam.

Tick boxes are provided for students to record their progress through the book.

USING A METRONOME

A **metronome** is a device that will click a regular pulse at any speed you wish to help you keep in time when practising. There are several on the internet and the one at www.metronomeonline.com is free and easy to use. The numbers around the dial indicate the speed in beats (or pulses) per minute: the higher the number, the faster the speed.

KEYS AND KEY SIGNATURES

 Grade 5 sight reading can be in any major key with a key signature of up to four sharps or flats, or in any minor key with a key signature of up to three sharps or flats. In the following list, the keys that are new for Grade 5 sight reading are printed in **bold type.**

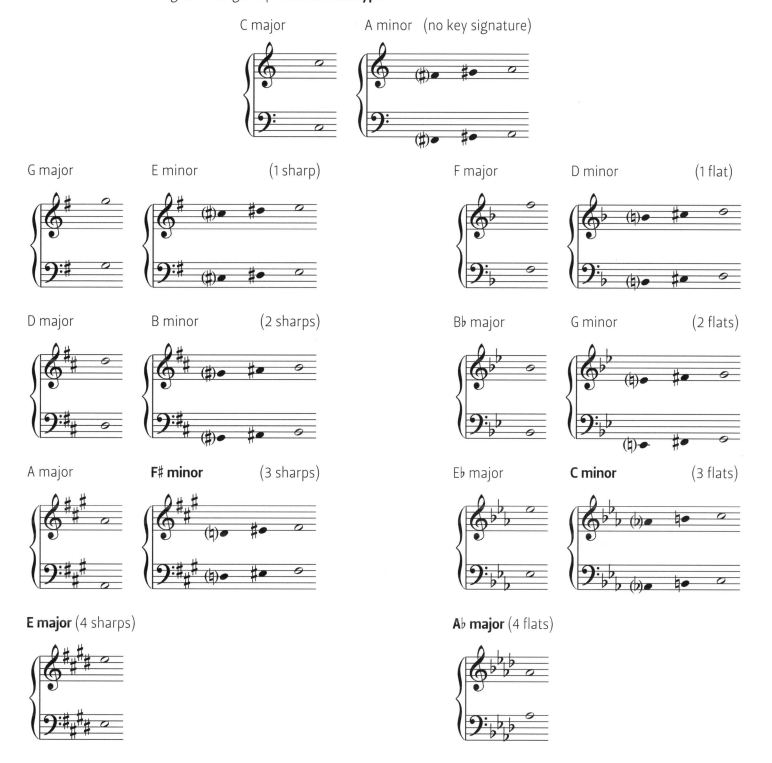

Remember:

-   When there are sharps in a key signature, the name of the major key is one step above the last sharp in the key signature. So, if the key signature ends with G♯ the major key is A major.

-   When there are flats in a key signature, the name of the major key is the same as the next-to-last flat in the key signature. So, if the next-to-last flat in the key signature is E♭ the major key is E♭ major.

However, each major key has a minor key that shares the same key signature. To check whether the key is major or minor, look at the last bass note in the piece:

- If the music has a key signature of one sharp and the last bass note is G, the key is likely to be G major.

- If the music has a key signature of one sharp and the last bass note is E, the key is likely to be E minor. In minor keys, you are also likely to see an accidental in front of the note that is one step below the key note, especially near the end of the piece. So, if the music seems to be in E minor, a D♯ just before the end would confirm that the key is E minor, rather than G major.

 Now try sight reading some short pieces in the keys that are new for Grade 5. The first one has a key signature of four sharps, and no accidentals. Because D♯ is the last sharp in the key signature, and there are no accidentals, the key must be **E major.** The black notes have been marked with arrows in the music.

First listen to the recording of the piece.

Now get your hands ready to play, using the given fingering as a guide. The right hand starts with the thumb on E and your fingers should hover over the first five notes of the scale of E major in order to reach B in bar 2. Remember to be ready for the black notes.

Your left hand starts with the thumb on B and ranges down the scale to E. Again, ensure your fingers are hovering over F♯ and G♯ for the key of E major.

Notice the printed fingerings in the right-hand part and try these out in advance. In the first bar, your second finger must cross your thumb to reach down to D♯, and there are some finger extensions in the last bar, although the fingering here should be familiar, as it is a standard E major arpeggio.

Give yourself a two-bar count in, and then play the piece for yourself.

3 The next piece has a key signature of four flats. The next-to-last flat in the key signature (Ab) gives us the name of the key and, although there is an accidental in the middle, the final bass note confirms that the key is **Ab major.**

Listen to the recording, and then try playing this on the piano. First try out any places where the fingering looks tricky. Then get both hands into position for the start, with fingers hovering over Ab, Bb, C, Db and Eb. Notice that all these are black notes, apart from C. In fact, there are far more black notes than white throughout the entire piece.

Give yourself a two-bar count-in, remembering that the upbeat start means that you should begin playing on the final '4' of your count-in. The pause signs at the end tell you to hang on to the last notes of the piece for longer than is suggested by the printed note lengths.

 4 **C minor** has the same key signature as Eb major (three flats), but it can also have accidentals for B♮, temporarily cancelling the Bb in the key signature, and A♮, cancelling the Ab in the key signature. The final bass note C in the next piece confirms that the key is C minor, not Eb major. Listen to this piece before playing it yourself on the piano.

 5 The last new key is **F# minor**. This has the same key signature as A major (three sharps) but it also has accidentals for E# and sometimes for D#. Remember E# is a white note – the same note as F.

After listening to this piece, get ready to play it on the piano. More than half of the notes are black notes, so try to remember the key signature. You also need to be ready for the extension to top D in the right-hand part of bar 3, and the small changes of left-hand position in bars 3 and 4.

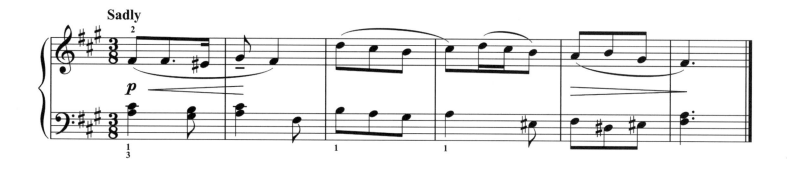

6

You are also likely to see accidentals in Grade 5 sight reading that are not part of a minor key, but have been used to add colour to the music. Sometimes they can create a deliberately surprising effect, as at the start of the second line of music in this piece.

When studying the music before playing it, try out anything that looks unusual like this – you don't want the effect to be so surprising that it makes you hesitate or stop.

TICK THE BOX WHEN YOU HAVE COMPLETED THIS SECTION ☐

TERMS AND SIGNS

 7

There are a few more foreign-language terms for tempo and mood that are useful to know for Grade 5. You can hear how to pronounce these words by listening to track 7.

Con brio	With brilliance
Legato	Smoothly
Marcato	Accented
Misterioso	Mysteriously
Preciso	Precisely
Sostenuto	Sustained
Gigue	A fast dance, often in $\frac{3}{8}$ or $\frac{6}{8}$ time.
Ritardando	Gradually slow down (usually shortened to **rit.** or **ritard.**)
Rallentando	Gradually slow down (usually shortened to **rall.**)
	In sight reading, an instruction to slow down is most likely to occur just before the end of the piece. If it comes earlier, it may be followed by the direction:
a tempo	which means return to the original speed

You might also see the sign ***ff***, which is an instruction to play very loudly.

The following terms appeared in previous grades, so it would be useful to revise these too.

Lento	very slow
Adagio	slow
Andante	fairly slow
Andantino	slightly faster than andante
Moderato	moderate speed
Allegretto	fairly fast
Allegro	fast
Vivace	lively or quick
Alla marcia	in the style of a march
Cantabile	in a singing style
Espressivo (or **espress.**)	expressively
Giocoso	merrily
Grandioso	grandly
Grazioso	gracefully
Leggiero	lightly or delicately
Maestoso	majestically
Mesto	sadly
Poco	a little (e.g. **poco allegro** – a little fast)
Ritmico	rhythmically
Scherzando	playfully or jokingly
Semplice	simply
Tempo di minuetto	at the speed of a minuet (steady 3 time)
Tempo di tango	at the speed of a tango
Valse lente	slow waltz (slow 3 time)

RHYTHM

 There are no new note lengths or time signatures to learn for Grade 5, but you may come across notes that are tied together, or rests that are grouped together, to form patterns that will need careful counting.

Listen to each of the following pieces before you play them on the piano. The first one is in $\frac{6}{8}$ time. The tempo is fairly slow, so you can count six quaver beats per bar – but notice that it starts with an upbeat, which will need to sound on the second 'six' of your two-bar count-in. Remember that *cantabile* means in a singing style, so play *legato* and sustain the tied notes for their full lengths. **Rall. (rallentando)** tells you to slow down in the last two bars.

9 The next piece is marked to be played very slowly. Many of the notes are separated by rests, so it will need careful counting.

In the first and last bars, the large leap in the left hand is an octave (from C to the C below). Try to get used to spotting octave leaps quickly as they are very common in piano music. Also, watch out for the dotted crotchet in the left hand of bar 3 – it is easy to miss that this is the black note A♭.

 **10** Listen carefully to hear how to play the 'jazzy' rhythms in the next piece. *Con brio* means 'with brilliance', but it is better to keep to a steady pulse than risk tripping up through trying to play it too quickly. Aim for clear contrasts in the dynamics.

From here onwards, sight read each piece *before* you listen to it played on the recording.

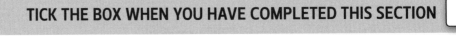

TICK THE BOX WHEN YOU HAVE COMPLETED THIS SECTION ☐

8

ON YOUR OWN

 Now you need plenty of practice in playing new pieces! The more you can do, the easier sight reading will become.

Work through the rest of this book, and use the recordings to check your playing. If you hear differences, try to work out why. Tick the box when you have played each piece, so that you keep trying new ones.

Things to check before starting a piece of sight reading:

· The time signature – are you going to count in twos, threes, fours or sixes?

· The tempo – how fast should you count? Look out for any pause signs or directions to slow down, and remember to give yourself a two-bar count-in.

· The key signature – which black notes do you need to remember?

· Are there any accidentals, and do any of them affect later notes in the same bar?

· The printed fingerings – try out any that look tricky, and use those given at the start to get both hands into position.

· The dynamics – where should you play loudly and where softly?

· Any legato, staccato, accent and tenuto markings.

· Are there any patterns in the music that will make it easier to read, and are there any leaps or rests that may be tricky?

Things to help you practise:

· Try playing slowly at first if that helps, and build up to a faster speed later: a regular pulse is more important than the speed at which you play.

· Try getting the notes and rhythm right first, and then play it again adding in changes of dynamics and details such as legato, staccato and accents.

· Try not to look at your fingers as you play, but keep your eyes fixed on the music. Get used to feeling your way around the keyboard without looking at it. Look ahead in the music to spot what is coming up.

Things to remember in the exam:

· The examiner will give you half a minute to look at the piece before asking you to play it. Use this time to try out the music – don't be afraid to do this, the examiner won't be listening! Play the opening and the ending, and perhaps any tricky bars. The examiner will tell you when to finish the try out and start playing for real.

· If you keep to a regular pulse at the marked speed and get most of the notes right, you will pass your sight reading!

· You will be heading for a top mark for sight reading if you also play fluently and bring out the expressive details of the music.

· Keep concentrating until you have given the last note its full length.

· **Try not to hesitate, even if you make a mistake.**
Hesitations and stops are the most common reasons for a disappointing mark in sight reading.

Good luck with your Grade 5 sight reading!

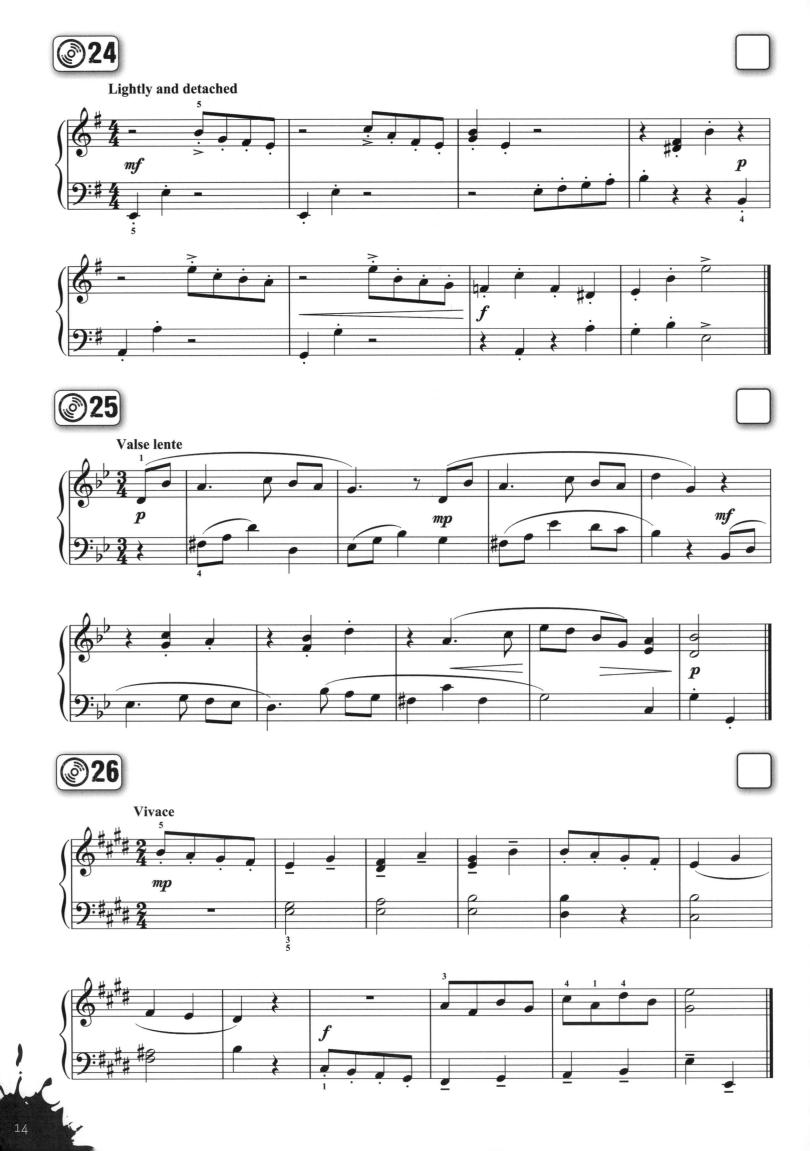

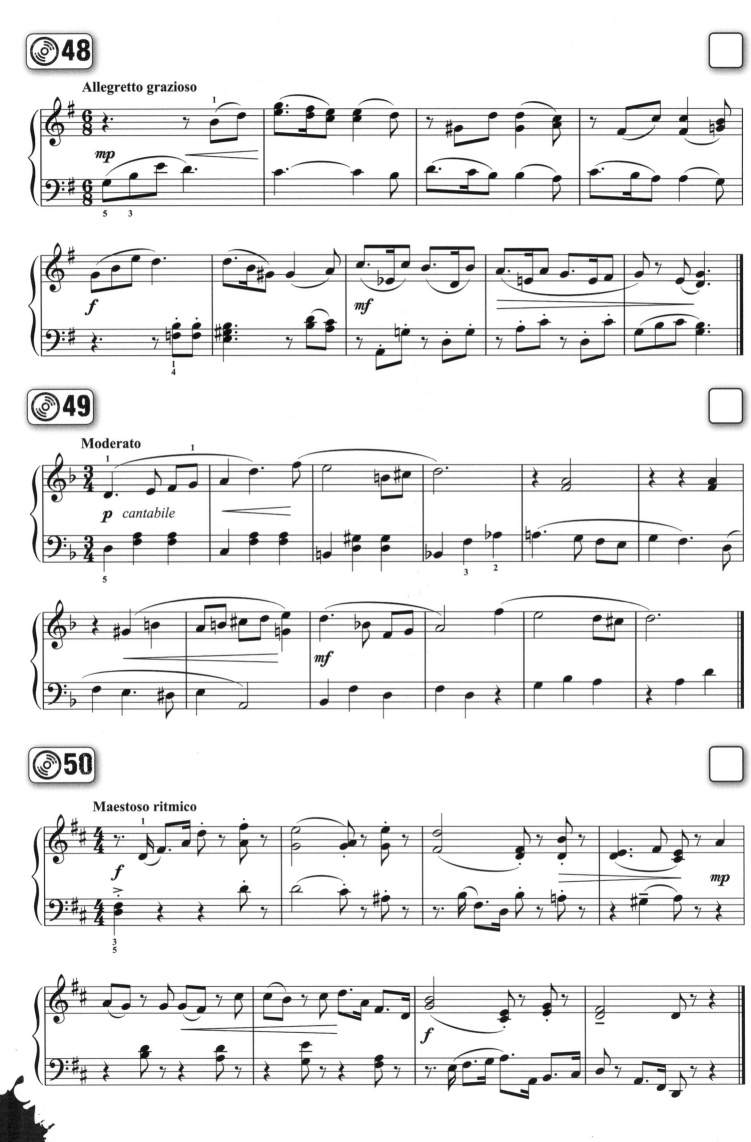

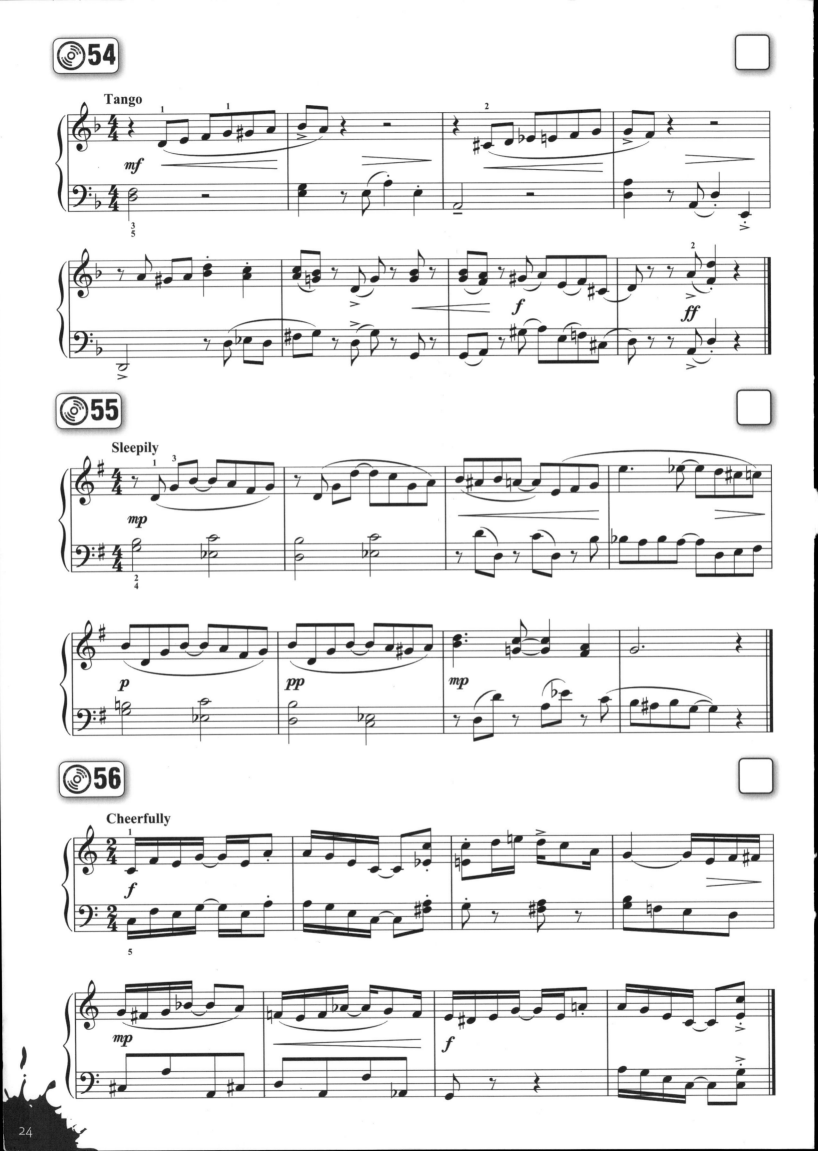